Countr

CIAO
from
ITALY

C. Manica

Ciao! My name is
Lorenzo Wolf.
I'm going to tell you
about my country,
Italy!

Where is Italy? Italy is in the middle of the Mediterranean Sea, in the southern part of Europe.

It's here!

Do you think it looks like a boot?

There are twenty regions in Italy, from Trentino-Alto Adige in the North, to Sicily (Italian: Sicilia) in the South.

Here are some quick facts about Italy...

This is our flag.

Our official name is Repubblica Italiana (The Italian Republic).

We have a president and a prime minister.

Our currency is the euro.

Our capital is Rome.

ROME

Our national anthem is "Il Canto degli Italiani" (The Song of the Italians).

Our national day is Festa della Repubblica (Republic Day). It's on June 2.

Did you know that I'm Italy's national animal?

Yes, it's true!

There's a legend that tells us how Rome was founded, and it involved a wolf. Do you want to listen to the story?

So, around 2700 years ago, two brothers, Romulus and Remus, were left in the forest as babies. A mother wolf found and raised them.

LUPA CAPITOLINA STATUE IN THE CAPITOLINE MUSEUMS, ROME

Romulus and Remus grew up to be strong and smart men. They decided to build a city near the Tiber River, where they had been found by the mother wolf.

Unfortunately, they couldn't agree on the exact site of the city, and got into a big fight.

Romulus won and became the first king of of the new city. He named it Rome (Italian: Roma), after himself.

Yes, Rome is around 2700 years old! So, if you like ancient history, you'll love Rome!

Let's go there to see some famous landmarks!

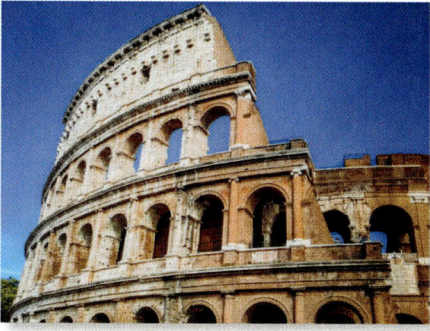

This is the Colosseum. It's a large amphitheater that was built almost 2000 years ago.

The colosseum was used for sporting events and games, including fights between gladiators and wild animal hunt.

It's so big, it has 80 entrances and could seat 50,000 people.

This is the Roman Forum. It was a busy center of ancient Roman daily life.

There were shops, government offices, banks, monuments, and temples in the Roman Forum.

This is the Pantheon, one of the best-preserved ancient Roman buildings in the world. Built around 2000 years ago as a temple, it's still in use today as a Catholic church.

Did You Know?

The pantheon has a huge dome. There's a round opening at the top of the dome called the oculus, which lets sunlight (also rain!) in.

Villa Borghese, Rome's central park, has gardens, playgrounds, an art gallery, a pond, a museum, and even a zoo!

Tradition says that if you toss a coin into the Trevi Fountain (Italian: Fontana di Trevi), you'll return to Rome. So, don't forget to do that if you really like Rome!

If you are super interested in ancient Rome, you can go to Ostia Antica, an archeological site only around thirty minutes from Rome.

Ostia Antica was a busy port in ancient times. You can still see the remains of warehouses, shops, apartment buildings, temples, baths, a theater, fast food restaurants, and even public toilets!

A THEATER

PUBLIC TOILETS

A TEMPLE

AN APARTMENT BUILDING

A SHOP

If you are super, super interested in ancient Rome, you should go to Pompeii.

It's an ancient Roman city that was founded in the 6th century BC.

After Mount Vesuvius erupted in 79 AD, the city was buried in ash and pumice for centuries until it was rediscovered in the 18th century.

TEMPLE OF JUPITER

You can see the well-preserved city and imagine what life was like in ancient Rome.

A FAST-FOOD RESTAURANT

PUBLIC BATHS

A MARKET

A THEATER

So now you know that Italy has a very long and interesting history.

It was once the center of the Roman Empire, a powerful empire that ruled over a large part of Europe, Africa, and Asia from 27 BC until the end of the Western Roman Empire in the year 476.

Another important time in Italian history was the Renaissance, between the 14th-17th centuries.

This was a time of great creativity and innovation. Artists created beautiful paintings and sculptures, scientists made important discoveries, and thinkers explored new ideas.

Leonardo da Vinci was probably the most famous Renaissance artist, scientist, and inventor.

MONA LISA

He painted amazing works of art, including the Mona Lisa and The Last Supper. He also designed many cool machines, such as the flying machines.

Other famous people who lived during the Renaissance were Michelangelo (an artist and architect), Galileo Galilei (an astronomer), Dante Alighieri (a poet), and many others!

GALILEO GALILEI

DAVID STATUE BY MICHELANGELO

A COPY OF DIVINE COMEDY BY DANTE ALIGHIERI

During the Renaissance, Italy was divided into many different city-states, each with its own government. One of the most important city-states was Florence (Italian: Firenze). It was (and still is) known for its beautiful art and architecture.

You can walk around the city center and see Florence's main attractions; the Duomo (Florence's cathedral), Piazza della Signoria, Uffizi Gallery, Ponte Vecchio (the old bridge), Boboli Gardens, and more!

UFFIZI GALLERY

THE DUOMO

PONTE VECCHIO

BOBOLI GARDENS PIAZZA DELLA SIGNORIA

Florence is the capital of Tuscany (Italian: Toscana). It's a region famous for its wine, beaches, beautiful countryside, and charming towns.

The city of Pisa, where the famous leaning tower of Pisa is located, is also in Tuscany.

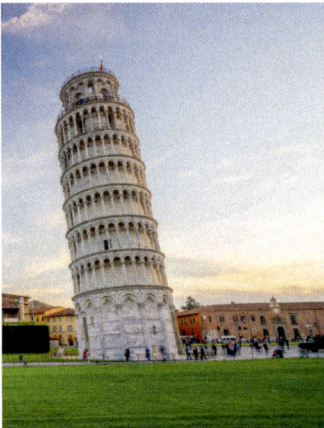

The leaning tower of Pisa was built over 800 years ago. It's a bell tower, part of a cathedral complex.

It actually started leaning when it was still being built!

Now, let's go to other places in Italy.

Venice (Italian: Venezia) is a very interesting city.

It's made up of a group of small islands connected by bridges. So, instead of roads, there are canals in the city. People get around by walking or by taking a boat through the canals.

There are different kinds of boats there; *vaporetto* (a public water bus), water taxi, *gondola* (a long, narrow boat), and *traghetto* (a bigger gondola).

Here are some famous places to visit in Venice...

ST. MARK'S BASILICA

THE GRAND CANAL

RIALTO BRIDGE

If you like nature, you can go to the Lake District in northern Italy. It's famous for its stunning lakes and majestic mountains.

Two of the most popular lakes in the region is Lake Garda, the largest lake in Italy, and Lake Como.

LAKE GARDA

LAKE COMO

If you love hiking, the mountains in the Lake District, the Dolomites, are perfect for you!

Now, let's go all the way to the South!

The Amalfi Coast (Italian: Costiera Amalfitana) is a stretch of coastline with beautiful beaches, charming towns, and towering cliffs.

From there, you can go to Capri, one of the most beautiful islands in Italy.

On the island, there's a sea cave that glows bright blue due to the reflection of sunlight. It's called Blue Grotto (Italian: Grotta Azzurra).

Remember when I told you about the ancient city of Pompeii? It's not far from Naples (Italian: Napoli).

Naples has seven medieval castles. Castel Nuovo (new castle) is probably the most famous, and it's located right in the city center. It's not really new since it was built in 1279!

Another interesting city to visit in southern Italy is Palermo, the capital of Sicily (Italian: Sicilia), an island and one of the twenty regions in Italy.

Palermo has a unique culture; a mix of Greek, Roman, Arab, and Norman cultures, among others.

Italy's climates vary depending on where you are in the country.

The northern part of Italy has cooler temperatures than the southern part. Winters are cold and can be snowy, while summers are mild.

The central part of Italy has a mild climate with hot humid summers and cool, rainy winters.

The southern part of Italy has a warm and dry climate with very hot summers and mild winters.

Now, let's talk about food!

Italy is known for its delicious food. Here are some Italian foods that kids like!

Pizza margherita has almost no toppings; only fresh tomato sauce, mozzarella cheese, and basil.

Pizza romana is thin, crispy and has a variety of toppings.

Cacio e Pepe is spaghetti with black pepper and Pecorino Romano cheese.

Arancini are stuffed and fried rice balls.

Gnocchi are small dumplings, usually made with potatoes or ricotta cheese.

Risotto is rice cooked with broth. It's creamy and yummy!

Polenta is boiled cornmeal. It's usually served with cheese or sauce. It can also be fried, baked, or grilled.

Panzanella is a bread and tomato salad. It's very quick and easy to make!

That's my *nonna**. She's a great cook!

*grandma

You can find a lot of yummy desserts too in Italy!

Tiramisu is a dessert made with layers of ladyfinger cookies soaked in coffee and mascarpone cream, dusted with cocoa powder.

Panna Cotta is a custard made with cream, sugar, and gelatin. It can be served with fruit, chocolate, or caramel sauce.

Cannoli are fried pastries filled with sweet ricotta cream.

Gelato means ice cream. You can buy *gelato* in a *gelateria* (ice cream shop).

With all those delicious foods, Italians need to do a lot of exercise to stay fit!

The most popular sport in Italy is soccer. Italy's national soccer team is one of the best in the world.

Volleyball is another popular sport. Italy's men's and women's national volleyball teams are also among the best in the world.

Cycling is an important sport in Italy. Giro d'Italia, a road cycling race, one of the three Grand Tours, is held in Italy every May.

Winter sports, such as Alpine skiing and cross-country skiing are enjoyed in the northern regions.

So, would you like to come to Italy? When you come to visit us here, we'd be happy if you could speak a bit of Italian!

Here are some useful phrases:

- ciao* (hello or goodbye)
- arrivederci (goodbye)
- buongiorno (good morning)
- buona sera (good evening)
- grazie (thank you)
- prego (you're welcome)
- mi scusi (excuse me)
- per favore (please)

*Use "ciao" with your friends and family. With other people, use "buongiorno"/"buona sera" to say hello and "arrivederci" to say goodbye.

Now you know a lot about Italy! What do you think? What's the most interesting thing you learned about Italy?

Bye, *ciao!*

Collect all the books in the Countries for Kiddies series!

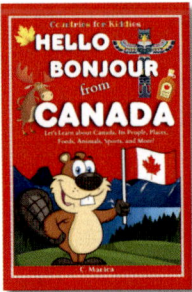

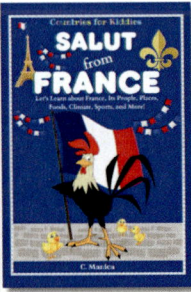

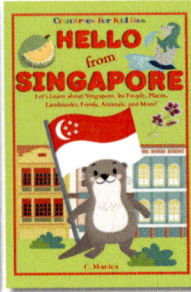

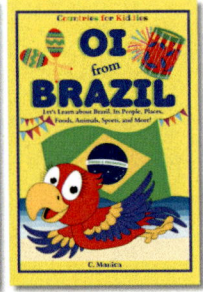

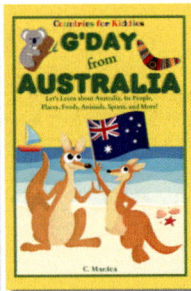

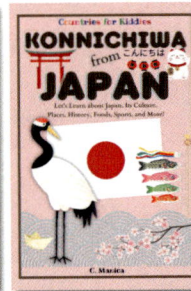

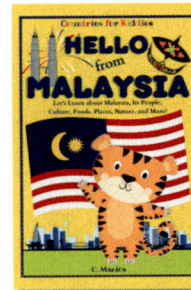

HELLO BONJOUR from CANADA

SALUT from FRANCE

HELLO from SINGAPORE

HALLO from GERMANY

OI from BRAZIL

HALLO from THE NETHERLANDS

G'DAY from AUSTRALIA

KONNICHIWA from JAPAN

HELLO from IRELAND

HAI from INDONESIA

HELLO from MALAYSIA

countries-for-kiddies.com

Made in United States
Orlando, FL
09 June 2025